The Kerry Way

Sandra Bardwell

Rucksack Readers

The Kerry Way: a Rucksack Reader

First published in 2005 by Rucksack Readers, Landrick Lodge, Dunblane, FK15 0HY, UK

Telephone +44/0 1786 824 696
Website   **www.rucsacs.com**
Email   info@rucsacs.com

Distributed in North America by Interlink Publishing, 46 Crosby Street, Northampton, Mass, 01060, USA
(www.interlinkbooks.com)

ISBN 1-898481-22-9

British Library Cataloguing in Publication Data: a catalogue record for this book is available from the British Library.

Designed by WorkHorse Productions (info@workhorse.co.uk)

Colour separation by HK Scanner Arts International Ltd in Hong Kong

Printed in China by Hong Kong Graphics & Printing Ltd

The maps in this book were created for the purpose by The Linx of Edinburgh © 2004/05 based on data from Ordnance Survey Ireland under Permit number 7944 © Ordnance Survey Ireland and Government of Ireland.

Publisher's note

All information has been checked carefully prior to publication. However, individuals are responsible for their own welfare and safety, and the publisher cannot accept responsibility for any ill-health or injury to readers of this book, however caused.

The Kerry Way: contents

Upper Lake framed by MacGillycuddy's Reeks

Introduction

The Kerry Way traverses Ireland's most spectacular mountain landscapes and passes the foot of Carrauntoohil, the country's highest peak. Throughout its 203 km (126 miles), dramatic peaks and glens, wild moorlands, lakes and windswept passes blend magnificently with extensive coastal panoramas.

Starting and finishing in Killarney, the route forms a loop tied by a stem to the town, resembling a walker's version of the Ring of Kerry road tour. Although coastal waters are often in view, the Kerry Way is largely an inland route, through remote and lonely glens, past lakes and over high passes, often following old roads and tracks in use for hundreds of years. It wanders through small villages, prosperous farmlands and the beautiful woodlands of Killarney National Park.

Highlights include beautiful lake views from Muckross House and Gardens; the secluded cascades of Torc Waterfall; oak woodlands – full of light and shade in sunshine, eery and mysterious in the mist; awesome views of the peaks of MacGillycuddy's Reeks; old coach roads above Dingle Bay, above the south coast and north from Kenmare; wide-open views from the ridges between Cahirciveen and Waterville; the mosaic of sheltered beaches, islets and rocky headlands of Darrynane Bay; and the tall, dark Dromore woods beside Kenmare River.

The Kerry Way is arguably Ireland's finest long-distance walk. And wherever you go, you'll find friendly, welcoming people with their uniquely Irish brand of hospitality.

1 Planning to walk the Way

Your Kerry Way holiday deserves careful planning. Committing yourself to the full distance of 203 km (126 miles) demands nine full walking days, three of them long ones of 28-30 km (17-19 miles): see Table 1 overleaf. This is more than some experienced walkers are used to. Aim to build in some flexibility, perhaps allowing for a rest day, especially in poor weather, or for a change of activity. A couple of spare days might make the difference between an enjoyable holiday and a test of stamina. Give yourself time to appreciate the scenery and wildlife.

If you have less than nine days to commit, there are various ways of shortening the walk using public transport (see page 9). And if you can spend longer, there are some enticing side trips, notably climbing Carrauntoohil (see page 17) or visiting the Skelligs (see page 45).

An important advantage is that the Way passes through many villages and a town where you will find accommodation, pubs, places to eat, and usually also a shop. So you don't have to allow for any significant walking distance on top of the overall total merely to reach and return from your overnight stay.

The Way makes use of a variety of routes: green roads, historic old roads, farm and forest tracks, and paths across moorland and fields. However, the Way also follows tarmac (bitumen) roads for about 38% of its length. This is more road-walking than many visitors might expect, albeit less than most other Waymarked Ways in Ireland.

The Way passes over Gortamullin, near Kenmare

5

None of the stages involves more than 55% on roads, and for five stages (1, 5, 7, 8 and 9) road-walking is under 50%. The prevalence of roads partly reflects the fact that in the past even tiny communities were linked by a track of some sort, and partly that rights of way are almost non-existent in Ireland, so it is difficult to secure access to land off-road.

Table 1 Daily stages for a 9-day itinerary		
Stage	km	miles
1 Killarney to Black Valley	22	14
2 Black Valley to Glencar	20	12
3 Glencar to Glenbeigh	18	11
4 Glenbeigh to Cahirciveen	28	17
5 Cahirciveen to Waterville	30	19
6 Waterville to Caherdaniel		
6a coastal	13	8
6b inland	29	18
7 Caherdaniel to Sneem	18	11
8 Sneem to Kenmare	30	19
9 Kenmare to Killarney	24	15
Total (coastal)	203	126
Total (inland)	219	136

✗ Changed

Fortunately the road walking is varied, almost always scenic and mostly along quiet lanes with little traffic. It also makes for faster average times than the off-road sections, especially those punctuated by frequent stiles. For safety advice on road-walking, see page 8.

Most people walk the Way anti-clockwise, turning west near Galway's Bridge towards Black Valley and the mountains. That way, you encounter the longest days after you're well into your stride. Stages 1 and 2 are of modest length, but they include the finest mountain scenery along the Way (and in Ireland). Should you need to curtail your walk, there are public transport options for returning to Killarney from Glenbeigh onwards, see Table 2 on page 9.

Elevation, pace and waymarking

The Way is generally a low-level walk, spiced with several crossings of ridges and spurs between 200 m and 300 m high. The highest point on the main route is at the modest altitude of 376 m (between Cahirciveen and Waterville). However, it undulates continually, and in the off-road sections obstacles such as stream crossings, stiles and fallen trees will slow you down.

Depending on the season and recent weather, several tracks and paths may be boggy, perhaps extremely so, reducing your average speed.

The size of your group is important: groups travel at the pace of their slowest member or slightly less. Overall, reckon on averaging 3-4 km/hour (2-2½ mph), unless you're particularly fit and impatient to press on.

The route is waymarked, mainly with black posts bearing a distinctive yellow walker icon and/or an arrow head and, in places, also a vertical splash: see page 41. Sometimes arrows or marks are painted on rocks instead: see page 6. Nevertheless you still need to watch where you're going. During the research trip for this book (May 2004) some crucial waymarkers were missing, obscure or hidden in bushes.

Having to climb stiles slows you down

In several places the route shown on official maps and in guide books has changed since their publication. Although our directions are reliable for the route as it was in summer 2004, official route changes are made from time to time, so you may have to rely on your own judgement and map reading. Vigilance is vital.

It's easy to overshoot a turning where the marker has been hidden by vegetation, removed or vandalised. Signpost arms may be twisted by practical jokers or by the wind, so don't follow them if they contradict the notes and your map reading. It's vital to detect a mistake quickly: if you haven't seen a waymarker for about 15 minutes, or if you reach an unmarked junction, you may not be on the Way. If in doubt, retrace steps and check your position from the map and printed directions. Note that North is tilted by 90 degrees on all drop-down map panels.

The Way passes among fallen trees

Mountain Code

To report an accident, dial 999 or 112 and ask for Mountain Rescue

Before you go:

Learn to use map and compass

Obtain the local forecast: see page 62

Plan within your abilities

Know simple first aid and the symptoms of exposure

Learn the mountain distress signals

When you go

Leave details of your route and check in when you return

Take windproofs, waterproofs and survival bag

Wear suitable boots

Take relevant map, compass, torch, food & drink

Be especially careful in winter

Steep terrain on Carrauntoohil

Taking care

The Kerry Way deserves to be taken seriously: it traverses exposed ridges and wild moorland. Even a minor accident can have major consequences, especially in sparsely settled country, where the nearest help may be far away. It's safer to walk in a group. If you decide to go solo, think how you would handle an emergency, remembering that mobile phone coverage is patchy.

The weather is a crucial factor, and it is unpredictable year-round: on any one day, you can walk through conditions typical of all four seasons. Rain is always likely, and it's vital to have the right gear: damp feet can cause serious blisters. Without good waterproofs, the risk of becoming chilled or hypothermic is high.

Make sure you set out each day with plenty of food and drink. There are shops at the beginning and end of each stage, but only on stages 1, 6, 8 and 9 can you pick up refreshments along the Way. Don't depend too heavily on the few shops or pubs, as opening days and hours vary widely. Some accommodation hosts will, with sufficient notice, prepare a packed lunch.

When road-walking, remember that Ireland has one of the worst road safety records in Europe. Large tractors often use minor roads, blind bends are common, and most minor roads are narrow and hedge-lined. If two vehicles need to pass each other, retreat to the verge, if there is one, and wait until the road is clear. A few fairly short sections are along busy main roads where extra care is needed. Wherever possible, walk on the verge side of the broken yellow line, in a narrow lane reserved for pedestrians, horses, cyclists, slow vehicles and parking. Although not completely safe, it gives some protection.

How long will it take?

The full distance of 203 km (126 miles) divides readily into nine day-long walks, suiting the spacing of villages with overnight facilities: see Table 1, page 6. Generally, little extra time is needed to reach accommodation. If you choose somewhere more than a couple of km from the Way, ask in advance whether your host provides lifts for guests. If so, it's customary to make a small cash payment to cover fuel, and you will be committed to a pick-up time and place. Ideally, ring to confirm arrival at the rendez-vous; there are public phones (coin and card operated) in the towns and villages at the end of each stage.

An official alternative route of 29 km (18 miles) for the Waterville to Caherdaniel section is worth considering (see pages 47-50). It's 16 km (10 miles) longer than the main route but offers as good a day's walking as any along the Way, passing through comparatively wild and remote country with wonderfully scenic views of the coast and mountains.

If there's a non-walking driver in your group, it's easy to arrange pick-ups as each day's walk ends in a town or village where there are designated car parks. Elsewhere it's difficult to find a safe parking place: leaving cars in passing places or in front of gates is extremely inconsiderate and almost certainly dangerous.

If time is limited, you could finish your walk at one of several points, returning to Killarney by public transport at anywhere from Glenbeigh onward (although some services are limited). Table 2 summarises the options; contact details for timetables are given on page 62.

Table 2	Bus services to Killarney		
Places served	🚌	Frequency	Journey time (mins)
Glenbeigh, Cahirciveen	279	once daily, Mon-Sat	50-85
Glenbeigh, Cahirciveen, Waterville, Caherdaniel, Sneem (Ring of Kerry)	280	once daily, Mon-Sat summer only	50-85
Kenmare	270	daily, Mon-Sat (+Sun summer only)	50

Check buses

Slí Chiarraí go Cill Airne
Kerry Way to Killarney

Slí Chiarraí go Neidín
Kerry Way to Kenmare

Travel planning

There are good transport links from Dublin (the most likely port of arrival for visitors) to Killarney, at the start of the Way. Irish Rail operates at least four services daily between Dublin Heuston and Killarney stations, with an average journey time well under 4 hours. Bus Éireann operates at least five services daily between Dublin bus station (Busaras) and Killarney, with an average time of just over 6 hours.

By road the distance from Dublin is 309 kilometres (192 miles); roads are generally good as far as Limerick, less so beyond. Journeys may take longer than you would expect as the main road passes through small, often congested towns.

Shannon airport, west of Limerick, is also a practicable access port, especially if you plan to hire a car. Another possibility is to fly to Kerry airport (at Farranfore, just north of Killarney) from London Stansted (1 hour 25 minutes) or from Dublin (1 hour); you can take a taxi for the 12 km from Farranfore to Killarney.

What is the best time of year?

Except for mid-winter, the Way can be walked in any month. Be prepared for cold, wet and windy conditions at any time, and you may be pleasantly surprised. There are several factors to consider before deciding when to go.

Winter days are short: there are only 7-8 hours of daylight in December, leaving no margin for error on most days. In winter, bus services are less frequent or non-existent and many B&Bs are closed. Side-trips such as an ascent of Carrauntoohil are unlikely to be feasible, and no boats run to the Skelligs (see page 45).

Midges and horse-flies can be annoying in summer, requiring precautions. During July and August, the busiest months of the tourist season, accommodation may be difficult to find without advance booking. All in all, the ideal months are May/June and September/October.

Responsible walking

The countryside provides many residents' livelihood; it is their workplace and your playground, where courtesy and common sense are the rules of the game and the basis of the widely accepted 'Code of Conduct' (see panel). The Occupiers' Liabililty Act 1995 obliges all who enter a farm to do everything necessary to ensure their own safety and to accept responsibility for any damage to private property, livestock and crops resulting from their actions.

Pass through farms unobtrusively and keep well clear of livestock, crops, machinery and farming activities. Your presence can cause stress to animals and jeopardise your own safety. Give a wide berth to cattle, especially cows with calves, pregnant ewes, young lambs, and ewes with lambs. Remember that it's a privilege to walk through someone else's property – follow the Code to the letter.

Walkers' Code of Conduct

- ✓ **Leave all farm gates as you find them**
- ✓ **Keep to the waymarked route**
- ✓ **Always use gates and stiles; avoid climbing fences, hedges and walls**
- ✓ **Take all your litter home**
- ✓ **Guard against all risk of fire**
- ✓ **Go carefully on country roads**
- ✓ **Help keep water supplies pure**
- ✓ **Protect wildlife, plants and trees**
- ✓ **Take heed of warning signs**
- ✓ **Immediately report any damage caused by your actions to the farmer or landowner**
- ✓ **Keep children under close supervision at all times**
- ✓ **Go quietly – avoid unnecessary noise**
- ✓ **Large groups are intrusive – keep numbers low**

 ## Dogs

You'll probably meet locals walking their dogs along parts of the Way, but the official advice is: 'Do not bring dogs on any section of the Way which crosses farmland. The Way crosses many fields grazed by cattle and sheep, and any dog seen chasing domestic animals is quite likely to be shot.' Access is a fraught issue between walkers and landowners. We suggest you avoid needless conflict and difficulties with accommodation and refreshments by leaving your dog at home.

Accommodation

The Kerry Way is blessed with accessible accommodation to suit all tastes and budgets. It's wise to book ahead to ensure that you don't have to compromise your preferences or your bank balance. Official websites and publications provide useful information: see page 62. Alternatively, sign up with a tour operator whose programme features the Way. Many will transfer your overnight baggage between accommodations: see page 62.

Many B&Bs, guest houses and hotels are registered with Faílte Ireland (the Irish Tourist Development Authority) and can be booked through the local tourist authority's website. At such places you're sure of high standards, including a private bathroom. However, some good B&Bs choose not to pay the Authority's affiliation fee; many offer good value though standards vary. These places are more difficult to track down for advance booking, but astute use of the internet will bring results.

To keep costs down, consider staying at hostels along the Way. An Óige, the Irish Youth Hostel Association, runs a hostel at Black Valley: see page 62. It has small dormitories, a communal kitchen and shop, but is closed between 10.00 and 17.00. There is also a hostel at Aghadoe (not on the Way), 5 km west of Killarney, close to the N72 road.

There are independent hostels in Killarney, Cahirciveen, Waterville, Caherdaniel, Sneem and Kenmare; the inn at Glencar has a dormitory but no kitchen. Standards vary widely, though strong competition drives out shoddy operators. Expect a bed in a dormitory or private room, possibly with private bathroom, and a communal kitchen; these hostels are generally open all day.

If you're happy to carry a tent, sleeping bag, food and cooking equipment, and to cope with bad weather, you can economise and be completely independent. There are commercial campsites with facilities in Killarney, Glenbeigh, near Caherdaniel, Sneem and Kenmare. Some hostels (and the Glencar inn) permit camping in their grounds – check beforehand. All Irish land is privately owned: ask permission to camp on fenced ground, and elsewhere, camp discreetly. You'll need to purify water – sheep are everywhere. Follow the widely accepted Camping Code: see panel overleaf.

Packing checklist

The list is divided into essential and desirable items. Note the value of gaiters to keep boots and trousers dry and mud-free. Also, if you haven't worn your waterproof trousers recently, test them before you go, when there's still time to re-proof or replace them.

Essential

- rucksack (minimum 35 litres)
- waterproof rucksack cover or liner(s)
- comfortable walking boots
- specialist walking socks
- waterproof jacket and over-trousers
- clothing in layers (tops, trousers, jacket)
- gaiters
- hat (for warmth and/or sun protection)
- gloves
- guidebook, maps and compass
- water carrier and plenty of water (or purification tablets)
- enough food to last between supply points
- first aid kit, including blister treatment
- toilet tissue (preferably biodegradable)
- personal toiletries, including towel if hostelling
- insect repellent and sun protection (summer only)
- cash in euros: cash machines exist at all overnight stops except Black Valley and Glencar; credit cards are not always accepted.

Desirable

- walking poles
- whistle and torch: *essential* if you are walking alone or in winter
- spare socks and small towel (for stream crossings)
- camera
- plenty of spare film/memory for camera, also spare batteries
- binoculars – useful for watching wildlife
- notebook and pen
- pouch or secure pockets for keeping small items handy and safe
- mobile phone

⚠ If you are camping, add: much larger rucksack, tent, sleeping gear, cooking utensils, portable stove, food and fuel.

Stepping stones near Galway's River

New to long-distance walking?

If you haven't done much walking before, it's advisable to tackle the Way with someone who can use a map and compass. Well before you leave for Kerry, do several day walks of at least four hours duration to test your footwear and build up fitness. Carry a medium-sized pack to become accustomed to walking with a load. Be aware that the complete Kerry Way is a major commitment, and not the ideal choice for your first long-distance walk. For advice on choosing and buying gear, send for our *Notes for novices*: see page 62.

Kilometres and miles, metres and feet

Throughout this book distances are given in kilometres and altitudes in metres. Irish road signs show distances in kilometres, but speed limits are still shown in miles per hour. The diagrams below may help with conversions.

A useful rule of thumb is:

To convert km to miles, divide by two and add 25%;

to convert metres to feet, multiply by three and add 10%.

```
0          1          2          3 miles
├────┬────┬────┬────┬────┬────┬────┤
0    1    2    3    4    5 km
```

1000 **3280**
900 **2750**
800 **2620**
700 **2300**
600 **1970**
500 **1640**
400 **1310**
300 **980**
200 **660**
100 **330**
metres **feet**

2·1 Geology and scenery

About 400 million years ago, huge quantities of sediments were deposited in south-west Ireland forming what we now call old red sandstone. Sea levels and temperatures then rose, and shellfish proliferated in the warm sea. When the sea eventually retreated, the shellfish skeletons were transformed into limestone which settled into a thick layer on top of the sandstone. These are the most visible and oldest rocks in the terrain through which the Way passes.

Next came a mountain building era, 340-280 million years ago. The sandstone and limestone were squashed, bent and pushed up, then eroded by wind and water. Most of the more fragile limestone disappeared, although there are remnants along the shores of Lough Leane and Muckross Lake near Killarney.

High parallel sandstone ridges took shape, one of which was the Iveragh Peninsula. This is the most mountainous of Ireland's peninsulas, aligned generally north-east to south-west, and dominated by the MacGillycuddy's Reeks range, with three peaks of over 1000 m. Its memorable name perpetuates a local sept (sub-group) of the O'Sullivan clan; 'reek' means a pointed mountain. Other local ranges, with summits up to 800 m, are almost as dramatic.

Hanging lakes in classic glaciated corries

Looking along the arête towards Carrauntoohil

The Kerry landforms were wrought mainly by a series of Ice Ages, interspersed with warmer times, which prevailed from about 200 million to just 10,000 years ago. Glaciers gouged out and deepened valleys and chiselled U-shaped profiles. They also excavated corries – small bowl-shaped valleys – at their heads. Where corries developed in adjacent valleys, the narrow ridges between were transformed by frost into spiky spines (arêtes). There are fine examples of these formations on Carrauntoohil.

The domed, grassed-over hummocks scattered across the wide valleys are heaps of moraine – the stones, silt and gravel left behind as the glaciers retreated. As the last Ice Age faded away, the land now lying beneath Dingle Bay and the Kenmare River estuary was flooded and the present coastline emerged.

2·2 Carrauntoohil

From the recommended roadside starting-point, start by ascending Caher (1001 m, 3-5 hours round trip). To continue to Carrauntoohil (1039 m and Ireland's highest mountain), allow a further 1-1½ hours out-and-back (4 - 6½ hours in total). To complete the entire horseshoe anti-clockwise, passing Carrauntoohil, you need a full day (about 6½ - 8½ hours hiking plus rest stops), as well as stamina and a good head for heights.

Warning
Between Carrauntoohil and Beenkeragh there is a tricky section of narrow ridge that demands good balance and can be dangerous in wind and rain. Consider both weather and conditions underfoot in deciding whether and when to turn around. Equip yourself for a strenuous, serious mountain climb (large-scale map essential; poles recommended).

The nearest access on the Way is from Glencar. To avoid 5 km of road-walking, try to arrange a lift back to Lough Acoose. At its northern end, continue north-east along the minor road for almost 2 km. The hike begins from the gate on your right marked 'Private: no parking', with a Kerry Mountain Rescue warning notice.

For the next 2 km, follow the steep whiteish 4x4 access road built for the hydro-electric scheme. It starts climbing abruptly north-easterly, but immediately swings right and continues steeply to a height of nearly 300 m.

After the road swings right again, its gradient eases notably, and you can enjoy over 1 km of pleasant walking. Approaching the hydro scheme buildings, pass through various gates to reach Lough Eighter (440 m). It points like a finger at the double lakes of Coomloughra and Eagher, which take centre stage in this dramatic amphitheatre. The photo on page 18 shows the ascent route to Caher from here.

You confront an awe-inspiring horseshoe of mountains that includes Ireland's three highest peaks. Beenkeragh (1010 m) lies to your left, Carrauntoohil's summit cross almost faces you, whilst Caher's three tops tower to your right. The ridge includes several lower tops, and the rock face drops almost sheer some 500 metres to the level of the lakes.

Walk south to cross the outlet stream, avoiding the wetter parts of the peat bog, then veer left (south-easterly) towards the right side of the horseshoe, climbing gently at first along the spine of Lyreboy's heathery spur. The gradient increases sharply as you approach the first of Caher's three tops by a precipitous, rocky path. The sustained, arduous slog to the cairn (975 m) is rewarded with lofty views of the horseshoe and the mountains beyond.

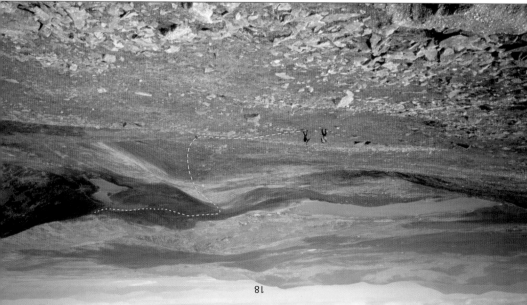

Yellow line showing ascent route from Lough Eighter

A rocky path of sorts take you down and up to Caher's summit (1001 m), then on to its third top (983 m). Be prepared to use your hands in places: see the photograph on page 16 (upper). Although Carrauntoohil's summit now looks more accessible, review the conditions and time available before deciding to continue. You are already enjoying a view that is almost as good as it gets.

Descending from Caher, the path continues around the horseshoe, sometimes dropping just below the knife-edge, and seldom as difficult or exposed as it first seemed. The ascent of Carrauntoohil is not as steep as the approach to Caher, and gives spectacular views over the lakes below: see the photograph on page 16 (lower). From its summit, the roof of Ireland, the view opens up to include the entire jagged ridge of the Reeks, with many peaks and loughs beyond.

From the rocky summit area, descend south-westerly to retrace your steps via Caher. Alternatively, if you have time and energy to spare, and enjoy rock-hopping at dizzy heights, consider the option of completing the horseshoe anticlockwise – but only if conditions are suitable. Descend almost northerly from just below the summit to continue the circuit via Beenkeragh and Skregmore before returning to the access road.

Whatever your chosen route, check your compass before leaving Carrauntoohil's summit, as there are several descent paths. Don't be tempted by the strong south-easterly path down to Hags Glen.

2·3 Habitats and wildlife

Birds and mammals are most active in the early morning and evening, so you're most likely to see them if you start very early or go for a wander in the evening. Midges also follow this pattern, so, between May and September, cover up and apply a repellent.

Greater butterwort

The Kerry Way passes through five distinct habitats:
- upland
- woodland
- coastal
- heath, field and hedgerow
- wetland

Upland

Most of the moors are carpeted with grasses and sedges rather than heathers and associated plants. Purple moor-grass is widespread, forming dense tussocks on damp moorland; it turns brown in late autumn and comes to life again during spring. Masses of bog cotton, with downy white flower heads, flourish in watery places. Here you'll also see insect-eating plants such as sundews, and an Irish rarity – purple-flowering greater butterwort.

Skylarks and meadow pipits soar overhead, filling the air with their melodious song, while the calls of black ravens and hooded crows are more raucous. Look out for kestrels hovering overhead and the darker, fast-flying peregrines. On lower ground you may also see and hear curlews with their long curved bill and plaintive call. Hares are quite common, easily distinguished from rabbits by their long legs and ears and bounding gait. Ireland's sole surviving herd of about 850 red deer roam the slopes of Torc Mountain in Killarney National Park (see panel on page 20).

Red deer stag

Torc waterfall

Woodland

Killarney National Park protects Ireland's largest areas of native woodland; the most prominent species are sessile oak, holly and silver birch. The trees, festooned with mosses and lichens, shelter ferns and small flowering plants including white wood anemone and bluebell. Unfortunately purple-flowering rhododendron has invaded large areas; it excludes native plants and is extremely difficult to eradicate.

On limestone soils along the shores of Lough Leane and Muckross Lake, alder and hazel are prominent in the diverse woodlands. When disturbed, woodpigeons take flight with a noisy clattering of wings and broken twigs. Look out also for the quieter robins and chaffinches: see photograph on page 22.

> **Killarney National Park**
>
> *Ireland's oldest National Park, Killarney was set aside in 1932 after the Muckross Estate was given to the state by its American owners (Mr and Mrs W Bowers Bourn and their son-in-law). It has since been enlarged to its present size (over 10,000 hectares) and extends from the northern shores of Lough Leane to the mountains south of Upper Lake, and from Purple Mountain in the west to Killarney in the east. It includes mountains, moorland, woodlands, lakes and Muckross House and Gardens. Several publications about the park are available from the small visitor centre in Muckross House, see page 23. For more information, visit http://homepage.tinet.ie/~knp* ✶ check

Coastal

Grey-backed herring gulls and the larger great black-backed gulls are common, not only on the coast but almost anywhere they can scavenge food. Along the short, coastal stretches of the Way you may see black cormorants, distinguished from the slightly smaller shags by their white cheeks and chin.

Fuchsia

Heath, field and hedgerow

In spring and summer hedgerows, marking ancient field boundaries and lining roadsides, display a wealth of wildflowers. Dense blackthorn (which flowers in March) and hawthorn (blossoming white from May) are most prominent, entwined with clematis and honeysuckle. They in turn shelter yellow primroses, pink and white wild dog rose, yellow-flowering cowslip, foxgloves with pinkish-purple, tubular flowers, and creeping thistle.

Vivid scarlet and purple fuchsia has spread vigorously since being introduced from New Zealand in the 19th century. You may be lucky enough to spot black medick, similar to clover and the source of Ireland's famous emblem, the shamrock. Growing in damp, sheltered places, its yellow flowers turn into black pods in late summer.

Wood anemone

Shamrock

Male chaffinch feeding on rowan berries

Large areas of open ground, formerly cultivated or grazed fields, now support spreading clumps of yellow-flowering gorse, bracken, and heather. Several small birds make their homes in hedgerows, Look out for the tiny, energetic russet-brown wren, robins with their red chests, blue tits and coal tits, blackbirds and song thrushes. Long-tailed, noisy black magpies are easily spotted in fields and gardens. During spring and early summer, the repetitive call of the cuckoo is often heard, but the bird itself – darkish grey, magpie-sized – is elusive.

Wetland

Yellow flag iris is widespread

Yellow flag iris is prolific around lake margins, and purple loose-strife, with long, dark pink flowers, thrives in marshlands. Early purple orchids, with long spotted leaves, are commonly found in ditches and poorly drained ground.

The mallard is the commonest species of duck, the drake distinguished by his glossy dark green head. Grey herons stand stock still for long periods in sheltered reaches, whilst orange-billed mute swans glide slowly and smoothly. Near streams, look out for the small dipper, with dark brown back and white chest, darting about and fishing in fast-moving water.

3·1 Killarney to Black Valley

Map	**panels 1 and 2**
Distance	**22 kilometres (14 miles)**
Terrain	**paved path to Killarney National Park; woodland and moorland paths through the Park; then minor roads and paths to Black Valley**
Grade	**steep climb past Torc Waterfall then easier ascent to head of glen; moderate climb up Esknamucky Glen; some descent then minor undulations through woodland (total ascent 310 m)**
Food and drink	**Killarney (wide choice), Muckross House (buffet restaurant), Upper Lake (tearoom), Black Valley (various, small shop at hostel)**
Side trips	**Muckross House and grounds**
Summary	**from bustling Killarney to the beautiful grounds of Muckross Estate, past Torc Waterfall to wild moorland and oakwoods**

i Muckross House and Gardens

The elegant Scottish baronial style house, designed by Scottish architect William Burn, was completed in 1843 for Henry Herbert. Prominent in Irish politics, he inherited the family fortune derived from copper mines on Muckross peninsula. With displays recreating the life of the Irish landed gentry, the house is open daily year round (entry fee). The gardens feature rhododendrons, exotic trees, a rock garden and a water garden. The traditional farms bring to life farming practices of the 1930s in Kerry. Mucros Craft Shop features pottery and other items made on-site and there's the buffet-style Garden Restaurant. For more information see www.muckross-house.ie.

Muckross House

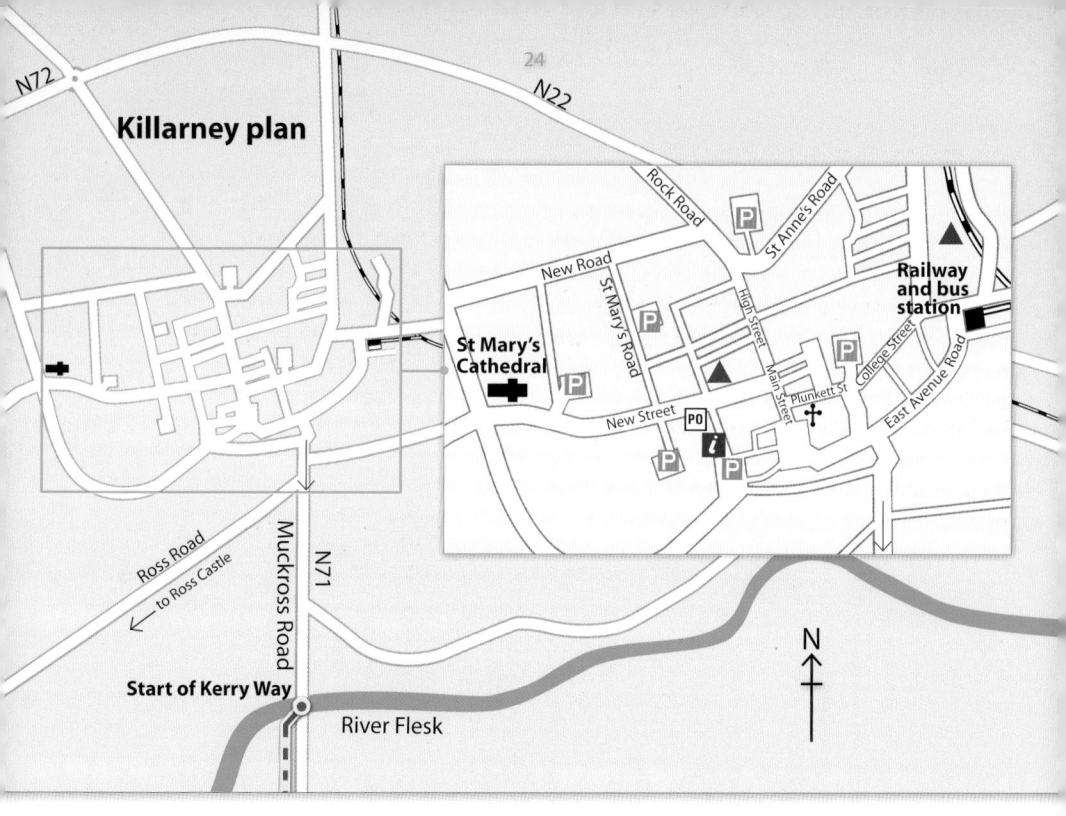

Killarney plan

N72

N22

Rock Road

St Anne's Road

New Road

St Mary's Road

High Street

College Street

East Avenue Road

Railway and bus station

St Mary's Cathedral

Main Street

Plunkett St

New Street

PO

i

Ross Road

to Ross Castle

N71

Muckross Road

Start of Kerry Way

River Flesk

N

Before you begin your walk, you may wish to explore Killarney: see panel. To visit Ross Castle, follow Ross Road 2 km south-westerly: see photograph on page 25.

New start
✳

- The Way starts at the Flesk River bridge on the N71 road to the south of Killarney, though there is no official marker. A wide paved path with fine views across Lough Leane leads to Killarney National Park, marked by a large sign: see page 20.

- Follow a tarmac path straight on through trees for about 250 m. Emerging into the open, bear right down a gravel path which swings left, parallel to the shore of Castlelough Bay.

---

i

Killarney

One of Ireland's most popular tourist destinations, Killarney is a bustling provincial town, with a central knot of narrow streets lined with small, brightly painted shops. Blessed with a glorious setting near lakes and mountains, it has drawn visitors since the mid 18th century when local dignitary Lord Kenmare developed services for visitors and built roads to link the area with the outside world.

One of its finest buildings is St Mary's Cathedral. Designed by architect Augustus Pugin and completed in 1855, it is a magnificent example of the neo-Gothic revival style. Killarney National Park adjoins the western side of town: see page 20.

The Tourist Information Centre (Beech Road) offers lots of information about the town, boat trips and Ross Castle.

- A few hundred metres further on and to the left are the ruins of Muckross Abbey, established as a friary for Franciscan monks around 1448. At a nearby path junction, you can go straight ahead to have a closer look at the abbey and surrounding cemetery. Otherwise, turn right towards Muckross House.

- Soon, make a left turn. Within 500 m the gravel surface becomes tarmac, which takes you to the threshold of the imposing mansion (see page 23). Turn right in front of the house and take a short cut across the lawns to the path close to the lake.

- At the next junction, with a stone boathouse nearby, bear left towards Torc Waterfall. A gravel path crosses open ground, with views of the steep wooded slopes of Torc Mountain (535 m) ahead.

Ross Castle stands on Lough Leane

Lough Leane and Sheehy Mountain

Killarney — 15 / 9¹⁄₄ — Galway's Bridge — 7 / 4¹⁄₄ — Black Valley

- Cross a minor road, and go through a short tunnel beneath the stone bridge carrying the main road over the Owengarriff River.

- Follow the riverside path past a stone building, a part-time information centre and source of light refreshments. Climb broad steps to the popular Torc Waterfall viewpoint – a beautiful series of small falls and cascades in a tree-shrouded gorge: see the photograph on page 20.

- Leave the crowds behind and climb up a steepish, stepped path to a T-junction, where you turn left. A short distance along, bear right at a gravel road, then just across a bridge, turn left at a junction.

- The track you're now following is the Old Kenmare Road, used until the 1830s. It gains height through oak and holly woodland to emerge into moorland. About here is your best chance of seeing red deer, though they are elusive.

- As the track crosses a crest, you may enjoy superb views north-westwards to Purple Mountain, named for its icing of scree, and the spiky peaks and soaring slopes of MacGillycuddy's Reeks beyond.

- The track descends past fields littered with small stone cairns into a secluded valley. Continue on a path through tussocky grass. Cross the Crinnagh River and a tributary by footbridges, then ascend through lovely wooded Esknamucky Glen by a wider rocky track.

West to MacGillycuddy's Reeks & Purple Mountain from Old Kenmare Road

- After a few hundred metres, a path of old railway sleepers helps you to cross very boggy moorland. Soon the descent starts, into atmospheric woodland of oaks and old stone walls wearing thick moss coats. Cross a small footbridge.

- Note the junction at a minor road: you'll return here in stage 9, on your way back from Kenmare. For now, turn right and after 1 km further reach the N70 road, beside deserted Derrycunnihy Church. Bear left for a few metres, over Galway's Bridge, then cross into woodland.

- A rocky undulating path winds through the oak and holly woodland so dense that you catch only occasional glimpses of Upper Lake below. After about 2 km, at water level, you're rewarded with superb lake and mountain views.

Esknamucky Glen

- Beyond the end of the lake, cross a stile to a path which bends right towards a large white house, a tearoom named for the long-gone cottage of wealthy clergyman Lord Brandon.

- Continue straight on along a gravel road, and cross a bridge with an arched gateway. Turn left along a minor road beside the Gearhameen River, soon passing out of the National Park. Ignore roads to the right then left, and press on to the scattered community of Black Valley.

West over Upper Lake towards the Reeks

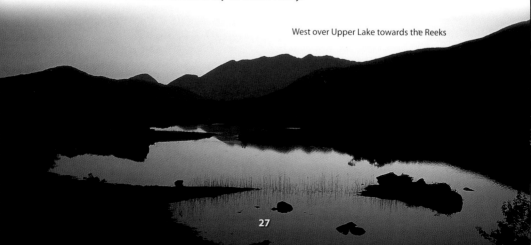

The Way at Dromluska

3.2 Black Valley to Glencar

Map	panel 2
Distance	20 kilometres (12 miles)
Terrain	quiet tarmac roads and gravel roads, forest and field paths; quiet road through Black Valley and Cummenduff Glen; old road and paths over a pass to a farm track and quiet road; another old road and path, quiet roads to Glencar
Grade	gradual climb then steep rise to saddle; sharp drop into valley; well graded ascent on Lack Road; steep descent into Caragh River valley; generally downhill to Glencar (total ascent 500 m)
Food and drink	Black Valley, Glencar (various, small shop at the pub)
Summary	spectacular mountain landscapes frame the crossing of two passes separating beautiful cultivated valleys and peaceful lakes

28

Lough Reagh, Black Valley

- The walk starts along a quiet road through Black Valley, past fields and scattered houses, with the precipitous slopes of the Reeks and the rugged Brassel Mountain towering above you to the right. On your left are the tranquil Gearhameen River and Cummeenduff Lough, with formidable Broaghnabinna (745 m) beyond.

- The tarmac ends after 3 km. Continue along a track winding up and around a plantation, through two gates. A path leads through the conifers to an open hillside, liberally dotted with boulders, waymarker posts pinpointing the route.

- Cross a stile to a green lane which zig-zags up to the right. Pass in front of a modern cottage and follow a minor road up Cummeenduff Glen.

- At the gate into a farmyard and prominent house, bear right uphill to skirt the property, guarded by dogs. Cross a low stone wall and veer left along an intermittently wet path beside another wall.

- About 150 m beyond the end of the house, ignore the waymarker pointing straight ahead and bear diagonally left through a gate, then follow an old track parallel to the fence and wall on your right.

The Way above the River Caragh valley

- This leads to a stile then a log bridge, possibly rickety and lacking a handrail. Follow waymarkers across boggy grassland then up through boulders. A path becomes clear and leads up to a broad saddle, keeping to the right of low-lying ground.

- Cross a fence and follow a path along the narrowing spur. It's worth pausing here to take in the views of the wide Caragh River valley and the range of hills beyond dominated by the tilted triangular peak of Mullaghanattin (773m).

- Descend steeply through boulders following yellow arrows painted on rocks. Cross a small stream and continue straight on briefly, then curve left down the steep, rock-strewn slope to a farm track.

- The next section of the Way may be unmarked: cross the fence in front of you, walk generally parallel to a stone wall, cross another fence then the stream below and continue through fields towards trees. Beyond another stream, go through a large gate and bend slightly right to follow a track past a farmhouse on the right.

- About 150 m beyond the gate, continue on a minor road for 1.3 km to a large stone house on the left and a Kerry Way sign on the right. Climb a stile and follow a tree-lined path up, through a gap in a stone wall, across a field to another fence and stile.

- Negotiate a small stream and bear slightly right to follow a line of posts along the old Lack Road, towards a rusty-roofed building. About 75 m short of it, bear right, crossing the remains of a stone wall. Angle slightly right, steeply up to the foot of the rocky mountainside where the rising line of the old road is clear.

- The road expertly deals with the steep grade in a series of long reaches between ten tight bends. There are some soft patches near the crest, where a stile crosses a fence. This is a great place for a picnic lunch, with magnificent views of the western MacGillycuddy's Reeks, Lough Acoose and the Dingle hills to the north.

- The Way drops steeply to the bank of Gearhanagour Stream. A path appears, widening to become a vehicle track. Pass a house at Derrynafeana and continue along a gravel road, over a bridge.

- About 150m further on, turn left along a minor road, which, as it climbs slightly, reveals views of Lough Acoose and more Reeks.

- About 2 km after the bridge, turn left at a junction (accommodation nearby) and follow the scenic minor road beside the shore of Lough Acoose.

- Beyond the lake and a conifer plantation, look back for a fine panorama of the western Reeks including Carrauntoohil, Ireland's highest mountain: see page 17. The road continues for a further kilometre to the Climbers Inn at Glencar.

East across Lough Acoose, towards Carrauntoohil

River Caragh

3.3 Glencar to Glenbeigh

Map	panels 2 and 3
Distance	18 km (11 miles)
Terrain	gravel tracks and short minor road to River Caragh; riverside and forest paths; quiet road across Caragh valley, gravel track around Seefin; minor road then busy main road into Glenbeigh
Grade	moderate undulations in forest; steepish climb to Seefin; generally downhill to Glenbeigh (total ascent 200 m)
Food and drink	Glencar, Glenbeigh (wide range)
Side trip	Carrauntoohil (see page 17)
Summary	the easiest day on the Way, combining pleasant forest and woodland paths, superb views of River and Lough Caragh and MacGillycuddy's Reeks, and vistas of Dingle Bay and peninsula

- From the intersection beside the Climbers Inn, turn left along a gravel road to head generally south-west down past rough pastures to a minor road.

- Continue straight on over the River Caragh bridge and turn right through a small gate.

- Cross rocky ground then drop down to *style* the grassy riverbank. About 500 m from the gate, cross a footbridge and go left beside trees for about 200 m. Then turn left across a log bridge to follow a path between conifers for about 150 m.

- Then follow three changes of direction within 150 m to reach a footbridge and follow a wide track through the plantation.

Larch 'apples' (young female cones)

- About 1 km further on, glimpse tiny Drombrane Lough through the trees as the track rises to meet a minor road. Turn right.

- After about 500 m, turn left uphill along a gravel track. Within 250 m join a narrow path which climbs to an excellent viewpoint eastwards to the Reeks, across gently rolling fields and woods.

- Steps lead to another viewpoint with good views of Lough Caragh and sprawling Seefin, the next major objective. Follow a path and steps through dense woodland and rocky outcrops, to a forest track.

Ragged robin

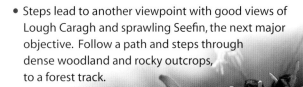

Glencar ——7——— Bunglasha School ———11——— Glenbeigh
        4¼   7

- Turn right, then after 300 m turn left at a minor road. Nearby on the right is a plaque commemorating the work in the United States of members of the Ancient Order of Hibernians. This Catholic organisation originated in the 16th century persecution of members of its faith. Its members raise funds for the benefit of their fellows and for kindred charities.

- The road passes through scattered woodland, crosses the Meelagh River and starts to gain height. About 1 km from the river, as fine views of the Reeks unfold, turn left at a junction near old Bunglasha School.

Windy Gap ← gotten

- The road goes up through moorland, past a plantation, towards Seefin's steep slopes. About 100 m beyond the end of the tarmac, bear right.

- The track rises steadily north-eastwards across the flank of Seefin, with spellbinding views across Lough Caragh to the mountains. Soon the sands of Rosbehy Point, then Dingle Bay and ranges of hills come into view. Continue downhill to a minor road, which you follow to the busy N70 road.

- Turn left along the main road, and walk the 2 km to Glenbeigh, taking extra care: sadly, there's no roadside path until you reach the centre of the village.

MacGillycuddy's Reeks and Lough Caragh from Seefin

3·4 Glenbeigh to Cahirciveen

Map	**panel 3**
Distance	**28 kilometres (17 miles)**
Terrain	**short road walk, then forest track; quiet road leads to scenic hill track; minor roads across Ferta valley, then field paths; brief road walk; hill tracks and finally 5.5 km along mostly quiet roads**
Grade	**short steep climb from Glenbeigh; long steady ascent; undulating descent into Ferta valley, one more climb, then downhill and level to the finish (total ascent 400 m)**
Food and drink	**Glenbeigh, Kells (limited range), Cahirciveen (wide choice)**
Summary	**forest walking along an old railway formation and quiet roads lead to an exhilarating traverse of a steep hillside high above Dingle Bay, followed by moorland and Ferta valley farmland**

Old coach road across Drung Hill

North-east towards the sand of Rosbehy Point

- At the western end of Glenbeigh, go right at a junction along a minor road, crossing the River Behy. Turn right at an intersection and continue for 500 m to a picnic area.

- Cross to a path on the right. Climb through conifers to a junction and turn left to gain more height. The track soon levels, following the line of a railway which between 1893 and 1960 linked Tralee and Cahirciveen.

- About 1.6 km from the picnic area, descend to a minor road. This rises gradually, affording fine views of the upper Beithe valley and the rugged hills to the south.

- Continue through a crossroads, and at the next crossroads turn left on to a road that bridges the main road. At the far end, turn right.

- Follow this minor road for 700 m to a junction on the left and go up a gravel track. Within 200 m you reach a gate, beyond which it's easier going on a grassed track.

- Eight gates punctuate the track as it rises across the steep slopes of Drung Hill, boggy in places. It follows the dramatic route of the old road, with magnificent views across Dingle Bay. If the last gate is locked, climb it at the hinged end.

Above the railway line, with two tunnels

- As you round a bend and head into a wide valley, look down to the right to see two tunnels on the old railway. A steady climb brings you to a saddle overlooking wide, partly forested Ferta valley, dominated by massive Knocknadobar to the north.

- Continuing downhill, there's a good view of the Gleensk viaduct to the north-west. Cross a small stream and follow a wide track into a plantation.

- About 1.6 km further on, a track leads across moorland dotted with peat extractions, soon with the encouraging prospect of Cahirciveen beside the wide Valencia River to the west.

- Past scattered ruinous stone cottages, bear left along a minor road for 600 m. Drop down right to follow a track across potentially boggy moorland. Ignoring intersecting tracks, go on to a minor road.

Gleensk viaduct

Valentia River

Glenbeigh — 16 / 10 — Kells road — 7 / 4¼ — 5 / 3 — Cahirciveen

- Continue along the minor road, after 250 m taking care to avoid turning right and uphill – unless you plan to finish the day at Kells, 1 km away.

- To continue on the Way, bear slightly left (the waymarker may be hidden in dense nettles). Continue for nearly 3 km to the second junction on the right.

- Leave the road here by turning left along a path between two large pillars. Pass through a small gate, cross a field then descend steeply to another gate leading to a lopsided footbridge over the Ferta River.

- Bear diagonally right across the next field, with a steep bank on the left, then veer left to walk parallel the river below. Cross a stile to the next field and go on to a solid bridge across the river.

- At a road, turn right and follow it for only 400 m. Opposite a large farm building, turn left along a gravel road. Go straight up to a junction where you turn right.

- A few steps along, cross a stile then go left up a field edge to the next stile on the right. Cross a small field, go over a stile and left up a gravel road to a house entrance.

Footbridge across the River Ferta *New Bridge*

- Bear right along a farm track to the point where the Way continues by turning left. However you leave the Way here to reach Cahirciveen.

- Continue along the track to a junction and bear right. At the next junction turn left, then it's only a short distance to a road where a 'Temporary Diversion' sign may direct you towards Cahirciveen.

- Turn right and follow the road for 2.8 km, past the grim ruins of a Union work-house behind a high wall (built in the early 19th century to provide shelter for poor people). Beyond a junction on the left, you reach the busy N70 road.

- Walk along the wide verge for 200 m, then turn left to follow a minor road.

- Cross a bridge over the Carhan River, then veer round to the right past the Memorial Park to Daniel O'Connell: see the panel below. Walk through the park to the main road.

- Cross the road and bear left, past a stylised sculpture of St Brendan's boat, incongruously balanced on tall struts. It commemorates the legendary journey of Brendan the Navigator and his companions who set off from the Dingle Peninsula across the Atlantic Ocean nearly 1500 years ago.

- Continue into Cahirciveen, partly along the verge, partly on a roadside path.

Monument to St Brendan's voyage

Daniel O'Connell

Born in Cahirciveen, O'Connell (1775-1847) is renowned as the 'Great Liberator'. He founded the Catholic Association in 1823 to win political equality for Catholics. Five years later he was elected to the British Parliament but as a Catholic was barred from representation. The upshot was the Act of Catholic Emancipation, providing highly selective voting rights. During the early 1840s he spearheaded a popular campaign for Irish independence. Although he was imprisoned for his activities and enjoyed hero status after his release, he retired from active politics and died a few years later. His home for many years, Derrynane House near Caherdaniel, is close to the Way (page 46).

Statue of O'Connell, Memorial Park, Cahirciveen

North along Coomduff Hill ridge

3·5 Cahirciveen to Waterville

Map	panels 3 and 4
Distance	**30 kilometres (19 miles)**
Terrain	roads and tracks to rejoin the Way; two long stretches of moorland paths separated by minor road walks; quiet roads into Waterville
Grade	an undulating ridge walk is followed by steep descent; another up-and-down ridge leads to the final descent (total ascent 760 m)
Food and drink	Cahirciveen, Mastergeehy (light refreshments), Waterville (wide choice)
Summary	a long, rugged and remote day with two first-class ridge walks and wonderful wide views

- To avoid repeating the road walk to return to the Way, try to arrange a lift with your accommodation host. Local taxis aren't available until about 10 am. If you have to walk back, after you leave the tarmac road (by turning left along a track) take care to bear right almost immediately, a few metres along the track.

- After 1.2 km, follow a north-easterly track steeply up to the crest of the ridge. Turn left over a stile and climb a broad grassy track to the ridge. Look back for lovely views of Cahirciveen and the Valencia River.

- The route is marked by black posts with the yellow logo and, in places, yellow arrows painted on rocks. A clear, intermittently boggy path generally parallels a stone wall and fence on the left.

- Cross a dip, climb over a fence, and then a stile. After passing close to the summit of Coomduff Hill, you descend, traversing a boggy saddle and ascending the next, unnamed hill. From there it's a fairly steep drop to a minor road near Coars School.

- A very steep climb starts the next section, up and over a minor bump. Then it's easier going, undulating over three tops and, inevitably, several stiles. The wide River Inny valley, with its typical patchwork of fields, moors, forests and scattered houses, spreads out ahead.

- One more uphill stretch lands you on Knockavahaun (371 m), the highest point of the Way's coastal route. Turn sharp left and descend steadily south-eastwards, with a derelict dyke on the right.

- Cross two stiles as the Way rises slightly over the last bump on the ridge. From here the rest of the day's walk – the long ridge beyond the valley below – is spread out before you.

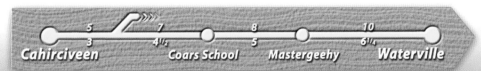

Cahirciveen — 5 / 3 — 7 / 4½ — Coars School — 8 / 5 — Mastergeehy — 10 / 6¼ — Waterville

Upper Cummeragh River valley

- On the descent, a stile puts you on the other side of the stone wall. Soon however, bear away from the wall to meet a farm track leading around to the left and through a gate. The track zig-zags down to a minor road.

- Turn right, then left after 700 m. The narrow road traverses the flat valley and crosses the River Inny on an old stone bridge.

- At a T-junction, turn right. Nearly 1 km along, at a junction on the left, you'll find refreshments at Mastergeehy post office.

- Carry on up the lane, skirting a derelict church to reach a minor road. Turn right for 300 m to a gravel road on the left.

- Walk past a cottage on the right and over a stile to continue on a wide track, wet in places, that rises steadily to the ridge crest. The waymarker pointing downhill marks the alternative, inland route to Caherdaniel (see page 47). To reach Waterville, turn right to climb steeply along the ridge.

Hedgerows add interest to minor roads

- The ridge narrows, providing an exhilarating walk along the crest to the first summit. The path is clear, but its direction varies over the rough ground.

- Descend to a gap, then it's steadily up, over three stiles and across a few soft spots, to the summit (Knag, 208 m). The sweeping views embrace Inny Sands, Ballinskelligs Bay and Lough Currane, contrasting with the mosaic of fields and woods.

- The descent includes three stiles and one minor bump, then continues downhill. Bear left away from the fence on the right, following waymarker posts down across rough fields to a stile beside a gate.

Statue of Charlie Chaplin, Waterville

- Cross the next field to a stone wall. Descend to another stile, following farm tracks past two houses and through gates to reach a road. Here you turn right and continue into Waterville. Beside the shore, you'll find a statue of the actor-comedian Charlie Chaplin, once a frequent visitor.

Lough Currane and Ballinskelligs Bay

3·6a Waterville to Caherdaniel – coastal

Map	**panel 4**
Distance	**13 kilometres (8 miles)**
Terrain	**roadside path and minor roads; green tracks and paths traversing Farraniaragh Mountain; minor road and paths above Darrynane Bay; short road walk into Caherdaniel**
Grade	**steady climb over a spur; fairly gentle undulations across minor spurs and small valleys (total ascent 330 m)**
Food and drink	**Waterville, Scariff Inn, Caherdaniel (limited range)**
Side trip	**Derrynane National Historic Park**
Summary	**an easy day with the sea ever-present, and superb views of inshore islets and the Beara peninsula hills across the Kenmare River estuary**

- Follow the main road south from Waterville across the Currane River bridge. A few metres further on turn right along a minor road and follow it for 2 km.

- Just short of a crossroads, the Way swings left, crosses a road and goes on up to the road, where it turns right.

- After about 600 m, past stone-walled sheep pens on the left, go left over a stile and walk uphill across a field to another stile over a stone wall.

- The Way snakes across the side of a wide steep-sided valley, where ancient field patterns marked by stone walls contrast strikingly with modern houses. There are a further eight widely spaced stiles to climb over.

- The route then goes over a rocky spur of Farraniaragh Mountain, down to a bridged stream and up a small grassy valley below the rock-sheeted mountainside, to a stone wall beside the main road. Climb the wall using protruding rock slabs as steps.

- Cross the road diagonally right and follow a waymarked track up to the crest, with a beautiful view of Darrynane Bay.

View south from the Scariff Inn

- Descend the grassy track, cross a stile and turn left along the main road. It's about 500 m to the Scariff Inn, which lays claim to one of the best known views in Ireland.

- Continue along the road for 75 m, then go down a minor road leading to Bunavalla Pier. Follow it round a tight bend, past a junction on the right and down to a stile by a gate.

- About 250 m further on, along a gravel track, bear left up a path to traverse above Darrynane Bay.

- After 500 m, there's a comfortable descent, mainly through hazel woodland, to the road leading to Derrynane National Historic Park: see the panel on page 46.

Skellig Michael

In the 6th century AD, Christian monks settled on Skellig Michael, the larger of the two precipitous rocky islands 12 km offshore in the Atlantic Ocean. Influenced by Coptic traditions from Egypt, they sought seclusion and isolation. During six centuries they built a remarkable group of chapels and 'beehive' cells. They left for Ballinskelligs on the mainland in the 12th or 13th century. Skellig Michael later became a pilgrims' destination, and is now a Unesco World Heritage site. Neighbouring Small Skellig is famous as Europe's most important gannet colony, and both Skelligs are rich in seabirds.

Boats sail from Portmagee, Ballinskelligs and Darrynane Bay and trips can be arranged from Cahirciveen or Caherdaniel in summer only, subject to the weather. However, landing on Skellig Michael is possible only under certain wind conditions.

Across Ballinskelligs Bay

Waterville — 7 (4¼) — Scariff Inn — 6 (3¾) — Caherdaniel

- Turn right then, 20 m further on, left over a stile. A clear path, boggy in places, drops to a stone bridge.

- On the far side continue down beside the stream for about 200 m, then veer left with a stone wall on your right. Soon you're overlooking Darrynane Bay.

- Scale a stile then, where the path ahead seems to be barred, climb around a makeshift gate. Continue on a level path to a minor road.

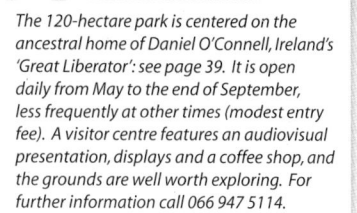

**Derrynane House
National Historic Park**

The 120-hectare park is centered on the ancestral home of Daniel O'Connell, Ireland's 'Great Liberator': see page 39. It is open daily from May to the end of September, less frequently at other times (modest entry fee). A visitor centre features an audiovisual presentation, displays and a coffee shop, and the grounds are well worth exploring. For further information call 066 947 5114.

- Go up to a junction and turn right. The road ends almost 300 m further on in a farmyard.

- Go through a gate ahead, along a field edge to another gate. Cross a footbridge, then go up across a small field and through a gap in the stone wall.

- Bear diagonally right over a stone wall, take a few more steps and cross another wall on the left. Continue through gorse. The track becomes clear for about 150 m to a stile, leading to a potentially boggy path with a stone wall on its right.

- Then it's up to a large stile and a path with a wall on the right. This leads to a minor road which takes you down to Caherdaniel.

Across Darrynane Bay from near Caherdaniel

3·6b Waterville to Caherdaniel – inland

Map	panel 4
Distance	29 kilometres (18 miles)
Terrain	minor road, farm tracks and hill paths to Dromod; minor roads lead to rough hill paths and tracks, then gravel road into Capall River valley; quiet road leads to hill paths, then old road to Caherdaniel
Grade	traverse undulating ridge; up and over spur; steep climb to Windy Gap; long descent to finish (total ascent 740 m)
Food and drink	Waterville, Caherdaniel (limited choice)
Summary	the most remote and challenging day, with a great variety of beautiful views of the sea, mountains and lonely glens

Isknagahiny Lough and Lough Currane

Waterville — 17 / 10½ — Capall River — 12 / 7½ — Caherdaniel

Lough Currane from near Cahersavane

- Try to arrange a lift with your accommodation host to the locality of Dromod, where the Way meets a road linking Waterville and Derriana Lough 6.5 km north-east of Waterville. From a junction here, the Way follows the minor road leading eastwards to Cummeragh.

- Otherwise, retrace your steps along minor roads, up to the ridge and along to the saddle north-east of Coomduff.

- Cross a stile and descend the hillside, initially on a narrow track, then after 200 m and beyond a stile, following a wider track.

- Continue down through a series of bends to a road. Turn left, then right at a fork along a minor road to Cummeragh.

- Just past a plantation, 1.2 km along, take the first road to the right. Follow it generally south for a further 1.2 km to a junction: turn right, then shortly left along a gravel track.

- Pass some deserted farm buildings. Turn left before a gate then right beside a wall. From its far end, go more or less straight along a track with a low wall on the right.

- After about 75 m, fork left and follow a grassy track up through bracken. After a further 75 m turn right, soon crossing a stream.

- Go on to the foot of the slope ahead – a long spur from the Coomcallee massif. Ascend a steep-sided gully following yellow arrows painted on rocks. Emerging onto the hillside, bear slightly right along a narrow path affording fine views of Lough Currane and Ballinskelligs Bay.

- Several hundred metres further on and beyond a stile, swing left to cross the crest and turn sharp left, with fine views of Capall River valley. A narrow path leads down through gorse towards some conifers.

- An old track materialises by the first of these trees, but soon fades. Bear right down through a gap in a stone wall and slightly left across the slope. Follow waymarker posts down to an indistinct track near a line of trees on the left.

- Veer left towards a farm house. Soon you meet a clear track: turn right and go down to a gravel road. Turn left and descend to a minor junction and turn right.

- The next 2.5 km are straightforward, down an attractive glen, passing an inlet from Lough Currane and crossing the Capall River to reach a minor road.

- Turn left along the road: the next 3 km is easy walking up a lightly wooded valley, enclosed by an arc of rugged hills. A rugged spur with prominent near-vertical strata overlooks Isknagahiny Lough.

Looking towards Deenish and Scariff islands

- Beyond a wood and modern house on the right, turn right up a vehicle track, shortly passing through a gate. Ascend through trees and across a field, bear left towards a large boulder, then cross a stile. Head left along a broad spur towards Windy Gap, prominent in the hills to the south-west.

- Cross a stile and climb a steep slope, passing through gaps in stone walls, across and beside streams and rocky spurs, and over another stile. Although the route is indirect, it is clearly marked by waymarker posts and yellow arrows on rocks.

- Then comes a steep section past a large bluff, over broken ground, now heading towards Eagles Hill (549 m) to the west of Windy Gap. Beyond a slight dip, cross the upper reaches of the valley for a few hundred metres.

- For about 250 m, aim for the bump east of the gap, then cross the grassy slope steadily nearing the rock-strewn hillside. A final steep pull takes you to the gap – at 385 m, this is just higher than Knockavahaun, the Way's previous high point.

- The descent, along a superb grassy old track across the steep flank of Eagles Hill is a delight, with a magnificent panorama spread out before you: wooded farmland and moorland below, the broad Kenmare River and the Beara hills beyond.

- After about 1 km, pass through two gates, cross a stream, then through another gate. The track narrows briefly as it creeps along a ledge below steep cliffs then, a few hundred metres further on, squeezes through a short passage. It drops to meet the main Kerry Way at an oblique angle, with Caherdaniel to your right.

- The wide track soon dips across a stream, then crosses a crest into sheltered Coomnahorna River valley, giving excellent views of Darrynane Bay with Scariff Island beyond. Continue steadily down through another narrow path, then some woodland, crossing one last stile to reach the main road in Caherdaniel.

Path descending to Caherdaniel

3·7 Caherdaniel to Sneem

Map	panels 4 and 5
Distance	18 kilometres (11 miles)
Terrain	hill and ~~forest~~ tracks and paths, minor roads for about 10 km; short section along main road; tracks and minor road to the main road in Sneem
Grade	steady climb, then gradual descent; steep crossings of two spurs; long gradual descent (total ascent 400 m)
Food and drink	Caherdaniel, Sneem (wide choice)
Summary	a roller coaster day across the foothills of a long range of mountains, with far-reaching sea and mountain views

The Way above Caherdaniel

Caherdaniel   12 / 7½   N70   6 / 3¾   Sneem

Above Caherdaniel, view south over the Kenmare River

- From the crossroads in Caherdaniel go straight ahead (east) along a path. Beyond a stile a wide track winds uphill, steeply in places, to the crest of a spur.

- The track dips then rises steadily to the junction where the alternative, inland route of the Way from Waterville bears off left. Instead, continue straight on, crossing a stile and descending on the wide track, which was once the main road between Caherdaniel and Kenmare.

- Beyond two stiles it becomes a minor road and passes the forlorn, overgrown Kilcrohane cemetery and chapel ruins. About 150 m further, go through two gates and follow a green track over a low spur.

- Then it's down into a valley, over stiles, through a gate and along a hedge-lined road. Where it bends right, continue straight on for a few steps, then cross footbridges over the Behaghane and Gowla Rivers just above their junction.

- Follow the track beyond a stile, with a good view of Eagles Hill and Windy Gap (see page 50) to the north. Pursue the track uphill, and cross a minor road to pass through a gate on a grassy track.

- Soon you're back on tarmac, descending into another valley. Near the bottom of the descent, look up to the left (north-east): in the middle distance, on the right of the upper valley, you may make out a massive grey stone wall, the remains of Staigue Fort. Dating from the 4th century, it is about 6.5 m high. Within 200 m, the road bends left: to reach the fort adds 4 km of extra walking (round trip).

- To continue the Way, go straight on along a wide, shrub-lined path. About 250 m further on, beyond a stile, the path widens to a track and crosses rocky, occasionally damp moorland.

- The track climbs steadily, dips across a streamlet and goes up through a short defile, to the crest of the spur: the view includes the narrow Bunnow River valley, the islands scattered about the Kenmare River and a range of hills to the north.

- Continue down the wide track beside a plantation. Pass through a small gate, go on for a few hundred metres to a small bridge then descend across a field. Cross a large stile to a gravel road, descend to a minor road and turn left.

- Scarcely 150 m along this road, continue on a fenced track. Cross a footbridge over the Bunnow River and soon start gaining height, steeply up to the crest of the spur and a plantation boundary.

- For a few hundred metres the driest route is through the conifers on the right of a boggy clearing. A bridge and stepping stones on the left then lead to a clear path down to a forest track, where you turn right.

- Continue to the N70 road and turn left. There's a wide, walkable verge for the 400 m to a minor road on the left. Descend this for about 100 m to a junction and bear right. The tarmac ends after about 400 m.

- Go through a gate, past a cottage and follow a wide track beside a plantation. Along here there's a magnificent view north across the Owreagh River to the cliff-lined glen east of the summit of Coomcallee.

- After about 600 m, continue along a minor road for 400 m. Where it bends right, go on through a large gate, along a track across the broad valley.

- From a left bend, continue straight along a tree-lined track. Cross a footbridge over the Owreagh River to a very minor road. Nearly 2 km further on, it meets the main road, where you turn left. Within 200 m there's a roadside path to take you into the attractive small town of Sneem.

3·8 Sneem to Kenmare

Map	**panel 5**
Distance	**30 kilometres (19 miles)**
Terrain	**minor road, vehicle tracks and woodland paths to the main road; tracks and paths, short stretch of minor road to Blackwater Bridge; forest tracks and paths; N70 for 2.3 km; minor roads, hill and forest tracks, then paths into Kenmare**
Grade	**relatively minor undulations; easy ascent then down to Blackwater Bridge; steepish crossing of Lacka Hill spur; short descent, then climb over Gortamullin Hill (total ascent 510 m)**
Food and drink	**Sneem, Templenoe (restaurant, bar), Kenmare (wide choice)**
Summary	**a superb day with a strong coastal flavour and leafy woodland interludes, finishing with two outstandingly scenic hills**

North-east from near Blackwater Bridge

Between Tahilla River bridge and Blackwater Bridge

- From North Square on the western side of town, follow the main road and cross the pedestrian bridge over the Sneem River to South Square. The Way heads off from the far left corner along a lane through woodland, bright with purple-flowering rhododendrons in late spring.

- After 800 m, turn left at a junction and go straight on at the next junction. Drop down, cross a small stream then regain height on a minor road.

- Along the next 2.2 km, the Way follows undulating woodland tracks and a moorland path. At the main road (N70), turn left for 600 m. Escape from it along the first minor road to the right.   → Passes Brushwood Studios

- After 150 m, turn left along a tree-lined gravel road. The next 1.5 km may be poorly waymarked and partly overgrown. Beyond a short stretch of minor road, a grassy track leads to a gravel road. Continue through a minor crossroads, along an indistinct stretch of about 250 m, to a gravel track.

- Cross a house entrance road and continue along a narrow path through gorse. Descend slightly to a large gate. After 100 m, climb a stile to a tree-lined track that may be boggy. Go down it, bearing left to a minor road, which you follow for a few metres to reach a junction by the Tahilla River bridge.

Sneem — 13½ / 8¼ — Blackwater Bridge — 6½ / 4 — Templenoe — 10 / 6¼ — Kenmare

- Turn left opposite a church along a minor road (signposted to Glencar). After about 50 m, turn right and soon you're walking parallel to the main road below. Ignore minor paths to the right and left in the woodland.

- Emerging into the open, pass a slender lake on the left. Within a few hundred metres the track widens through woodland, then rises to cross a broad moorland saddle. Descend gradually to a stile by a gate and go on to a minor road.

- This takes you past several large homes in spacious grounds. After 600 m, bear left at an oblique junction. Beware: the waymarker is easily missed.

- The narrow road becomes a gravel track after barely 200 m. After a further 250 m, leave it on a slight left bend. Descend across boggy ground, then go up a sparsely waymarked path to a saddle.

- Follow posts downhill, across a stile and along a clear path into woodland. Continue losing height, taking care to follow left and right turns, to a large stile.

- About 30 m further on you reach a vehicle track. Go left down to a stile, then right along a minor road to Blackwater Bridge on the N70.

- Continue south along the road for about 200 m to a forest track with a barrier on the right. After a few hundred metres, turn right down a path to the shore, a delightful spot with beautiful views of the Beara peninsula.

- The path wanders up and down through dense oak woodland, by the shore and slightly inland for several hundred metres. A steep rise takes you up to a gravel track: turn right and continue to a junction where you turn right again.

Kenmare River from near Blackwater Bridge

- Soon, beyond the end of a high stone wall on the right, you glimpse two large stone mansions at the site of Dromore Castle. After several hundred metres, pass a track to the left, then look carefully for a path to the right – the waymarker is obscure.

- The path takes you to a wide gravel drive which you follow left for about 400 m to another obscurely marked turn, this time to the right.

- After 200 m, turn left. Beyond the ornate entrance to a modern castle, turn left at a junction and continue to the N70 where you turn right.

- There's nothing for it but to walk along the main road for 2.5 km to Templenoe. Along here you could pause at a fine restaurant in a former church (which serves light refreshments), or at Spillane's Bar.

Kenmare estuary

- Further on, beyond a disused church on the left, turn left at a crossroads up a minor road. Follow it for about 300 m, then turn right through a gateway to a gravel track. This leads up to a locked gate, bearing the landowner's list of rules walkers must obey unfailingly.

- If the adjacent stile is inaccessible, climb the gate at its hinged end. Bear left along the field edge, gaining height. About 100 m short of a wooded area, veer right, following posts which could be elusive in poor visibility. On the crest of a spur from Lacka Hill, magnificent views open up of the Kenmare River and the Beara peninsula.

- Cross a stile to a rough track through a plantation. Cross another stile on the right where the plantation ends to tackle a rough, boggy track. After about 200 m, bear left to follow waymarker posts down a tussocky slope.

- Climb a stile into a plantation where you may have to dodge past fallen trees. Cross a stile, then a footbridge spanning the Reen River to a private road.

- This leads to a minor road where there's a camping ground to the right. The Way turns left, uphill for about 100 m, then turns right over a stile.

- After about 200 m cross another stile to open moorland and go on up to another stile. A few steps to the left, then it's right for several hundred metres.

- At the second stile, cross the fence on the right, changing direction slightly. Soon you're just about on the top of Gortamullin, a superb viewpoint, taking in the vast Kenmare estuary and countless mountains to the north.

- Descend eastwards for about 200 m, then bear right across a shallow valley. Rise slightly, then descend across the hillside following prominent waymarker posts, towards farm buildings. Bear right over a stile, then left over another after 200 m. Go down a narrow path to a minor road.

Church of the Holy Cross, Kenmare

- Continue down to the N70 where you turn left along a roadside path (unless you're staying at one of the B&Bs at this junction). Shortly, cross the road opposite the entrance to the Kenmare Bay Hotel, and after about 60 m turn right through a gap in the wall.

- A gravel path leads to a minor road, which you follow down to a footbridge over the Finnihy River. Go on to a spacious market square in Kenmare. Keep left, cross a road and continue to the Old Killarney Road junction, with a fenced park on the right.

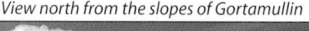

View north from the slopes of Gortamullin

Map	panels 5, 2 and 1
Distance	**24 kilometres (15 miles)**
Terrain	**roadside paths; minor roads across Strickeen Hill; tracks and paths from Windy Gap to Torc Mountain; steps and paths past Torc Waterfall and through Muckross Estate; finally paved path**
Grade	**mostly steep climb across Strickeen Hill; steep descent then steady climb to Windy Gap; fairly easy descent; up and down to Crinnagh valley, finally up and down again (total ascent 580 m)**
Food and drink	**Kenmare, Muckross House, Killarney**
Summary	**through farmland, over a high gap then through the beautiful woods and wild moors of Killarney National Park, leading to the grounds of Muckross House with wide lake views**

Oakwood above Galway's River

Kenmare — 10 / 6¼ — **Kerry Way junction** — 14 / 8¾ — **Killarney**

Old Killarney Road towards Windy Gap

- From The Square, follow the roadside footpath northwards along Old Killarney Road. Pass the impressive Holy Cross Church (see page 58), then ignore junctions on the left and right. As you start to climb, the path ends and you're walking on the road itself, though mercifully it's very quiet.

- The road rises steeply across the eastern flank of Strickeen Hill, to a saddle. The view is dominated by a long range of hills with your next objective, another Windy Gap, directly ahead.

- The road descends steeply to a bridge then rises to a crossroads. Continue straight along a gravel track (once the road to Killarney); it climbs steadily except for one minor dip. The steep slopes of Peakeen Mountain and Knockanaguish to the left and right close in as you approach Windy Gap, which affords fine views of Purple Mountain.

- Descend the rocky track and cross three streams where the stepping stones could be submerged after rain. Continue past tall conifers on the left hiding the ruins of a substantial house.

- Then come another three stream crossings on stepping stones; the second one requires good balance when taking the first step. Shortly you're on a minor road, for just 250 m, to the path junction you passed days ago en route to Black Valley: see page 27, second bullet. The summary below may jog your memory.

- Go up through the oakwood, over a crest, down through woodland, then across a wide, flat valley. A broad track then takes you up, across the slopes of Torc Mountain and down into woodland. Bear right at a fork, then cross a bridge.

- Opposite a car park, descend to Torc Waterfall. Afterwards keep left past a small stone building and go through a tunnel under the road. Soon cross a minor road and follow a path signposted to Muckross House.

- At a junction (where the Arboretum is to the right), follow a road for just 200 m and bear left, towards Killarney. Swing right at the next junction, or cut across the lawns to the entrance to Muckross House.

- Follow the road straight on from the front of the house. At a crossroads take the path to the right (signposted to Killarney) for a few hundred metres to a road. Cross it to a narrow path between the road and lake shore.

- This joins a wider path opposite Muckross Abbey. Follow a path round to the right and up to a minor road, where you turn left. This road soon becomes the footpath parallel to the N70. Within 2 km, at Flesk Bridge, you complete the Way.

Sheehy Mountain from Muckross Lake

4 Reference

Contact details

Telephone numbers are shown in international form. Within Ireland, replace the country code (00 353) with an 0 before dialling the number.

Cork Kerry Tourism, the official tourist body for county Kerry, has a useful website: **www.corkkerry.ie** on which you can book accommodation (or phone 00 353 21 425 5100). Locally, Killarney Information Centre, Beech Rd (tel 00 353 64 31 633) is open all year. The four-language website **www.irishwaymarkedways.ie** has basic details of all Irish Ways.

Hostels and camping

An Óige (Irish Youth Hostel Association) is at 61 Mountjoy St, Dublin 7 (tel 00 353 1 830 4555, fax 1 830 5808). Its website (**www.anoige.ie**) has details of all its hostels and offers online booking. In addition to Dublin and Cork, there are hostels locally near Killarney and at Black Valley. Membership (optional) entitles you to discounts on overnight fees, travel and much else. Overnight charges vary according to location and season, in 2004 ranging from €14 (Black Valley, low season, over-18s) to €20 (Dublin, high season, adult, including continental breakfast).

Several independent hostels are on or close to the Way: details from Independent Holiday Hostels of Ireland, 57 Lower Gardiner St, Dublin 1, tel 00 353 1 836 4700, or from **www.hostels-ireland.com**.

The annual guide published by the Irish Caravan & Camping Council, PO Box 4443, Dublin 2 (fax 00 353 98 28237, **www.camping-ireland.ie**) gives detailed campsite listings. Prices vary: in 2004, a site in Killarney charged €5.50 for a hiker with tent. There are designated campsites on or near the Way at Killarney, Glenbeigh, Cahirciveen, Caherdaniel, Sneem and Kenmare. Some hostels allow camping in their grounds: ask beforehand.

Weather forecasts

Met Éireann (Ireland's weather office) has a helpful website at **www.meteireann.ie** – click on Munster. Or phone Weatherdial on 1550 123 850 (Munster); calls cost €0.95 per minute.

Transport

Aer Lingus   **www.aerlingus.com**
tel 0845 084 4444 (UK)

British Airways   **www.ba.com**
tel 0845 773 3377 (UK)

Ryanair   **www.ryanair.com**
tel 0871 246 0000 (UK)

Aer Arann   **www.aerarann.com**
tel 0800 587 2324 (UK)

Dublin Airport   **www.dublinairport.com**
tel 00 353 1 814 1111

Kerry Airport   **www.kerryairport.ie**
tel 00 353 66 976 4350

Irish Ferries   **www.irishferries.com**
tel 0870 517 1717 (UK)

Stena Line   **www.stenaline.com**
tel 0870 570 7070 (UK)

Dublin Bus   **www.dublinbus.ie**
tel 00 353 8 872 0000

Bus Éireann   **www.buseireann.ie**
tel 00 353 1 836 6111

Iarnrod Éireann (Irish Rail)
tel 00 353 1 836 6222
                          www.irishrail.ie

Guided walks/baggage transfer

Irish Ways   **www.irishways.com**
tel 00 44 1730 71041 (UK)

SouthWest Walks
              www.southwestwalksireland.com
tel 00 353 66712 8733

Trek-Inn Holidays   **www.trek-inn.com**
tel 00 44 7005 803364 (UK)

Notes for novices

If you're new to long-distance walking, you may find our notes on preparation and gear helpful. They are available free to website visitors from **www.rucsacs.com**. If you don't have Internet access, send a suitably stamped, addressed envelope marked *Notes for novices,* to: Rucksack Readers, Landrick Lodge, Dunblane, FK15 0HY, UK.

Maps

The Ordnance Survey Ireland Discovery Series (1:50,000) covers the Way with sheets 70, 78, 83, 84 and 85. Most are dated 2000, but sheet 83 was revised in 2002. Several route changes have been made since, all of which (as of 2004) are shown on our drop-down map. OSI maps are also available laminated and waterproof, but these are much more expensive. OSI maps are available at the Tourist Information Centre and shops in Killarney, or direct from **www.irishmaps.ie**.

Further reading

Bardwell, S et al *Walking in Ireland* Lonely Planet, 368 pp, 2003, 1-86450-323-8

Comprehensive and reliable; useful for planning extended and day walks (2nd edition)

Corcoran, Kevin *Kerry Walks* O'Brien, 160 pp, 2001, 0-86278-744-0

Well written and highly informative; very useful for day walks in the area (revised edition)

Lavelle, Des *The Skellig Story* O'Brien, 90 pp, 2004, 0-86278-882-X

The Skelligs revealed by a local resident, seaman, diver and photographer; excellent on monastic history and wildlife above and below water.

Acknowledgements

Grateful thanks to Helen and Gareth for advice about Carrauntoohil; to Hal for support throughout; and to Jetta for companionship, advice and support during the walk.

Photo credits

Sandra Bardwell p4, p7 (middle), p14, p16 (lower), p19 (upper), p21 (lower), p23, p25 (lower), p26, p27 (upper), p28, p29, p30, p32, p33 (lower), p34, p35, p37 (both), p38, p39 (lower), p40, p41, p42 (upper), p43 (lower), p46, p47, p48 (upper), p51, p54, p55, p57, p59, p60; **Peter Cairns**/rspb-images.com p19 (lower); **Mike Lane**/rspb-images.com p22 (upper); **Gareth McCormack** front cover; **Jacquetta Megarry** title page, p5, p6, p7 (upper and lower), p8, p10/11, p15, p16 (upper), p20, p21 (upper and middle), p22 (lower), p25 (upper), p27 (lower), p31 (both), p33 (upper), p36 (both), p39 (upper), p42 (lower), p43 (upper), p44, p45, p48 (upper), p49, p50, p52, p53, p56, p58 (both), p61, back cover

More from Rucksack Readers

The titles below cover long-distance walks worldwide and in Ireland (top row) and in the Highlands of Scotland (bottom row).

ISBN 1-898481-12-1

ISBN 1-898481-16-4

ISBN 1-898481-17-2

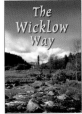

ISBN 1-898481-14-8

ISBN 1-898481-18-0

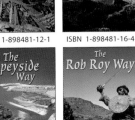

ISBN 1-898481-08-3

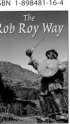

ISBN 1-898481-13-X

ISBN 1-898481-15-6

ISBN 1-898481-19-9

ISBN 1-898481-21-0

For more information, or to order, visit **www.rucsacs.com** or telephone: 01786 824 696 (+44 1786 824 696)

Index